TOP TIPS:
DEVELOPING
PARTNERSHIPS BETWEEN
CHURCH AND SCHOOL

Alan Charter and Gill Marchant

The right of Alan Charter and Gill
Marchant to be identified as authors
of this work has been asserted by
them in accordance with the
Copyright, Designs and Patents Act
1988.

British Library Cataloguing-in-
Publication Data: a catalogue record
of this book is available from the
British Library.

Printed and bound in Singapore by
Tien Wah Press Ltd

Logo, cover design, internal design:
www.splash-design.co.uk

Internal illustrations: Colin Smithson

Typesetting: Richard Jefferson, Author
and Publisher Services

Consultants: Liz Green, Lisa Jones,
Nigel Roberts

✦ Scripture Union is an
international Christian charity working
with churches in more than 130
countries, providing resources to bring
the good news about Jesus Christ to
children, young people and families
and to encourage them to develop
spiritually through the Bible and
prayer.

As well as our network of volunteers,
staff and associates who run holidays,
church-based events and school
Christian groups, we produce a wide
range of publications and support
those who use our resources through
training programmes.

CONTENTS

INTRODUCTION

Jesus believed that every child matters! Over the centuries, to the present day, individual Christians, churches and organisations, inspired by this belief, have worked for the interests of children in society. But Government has now recognised the need to provide extra child-focused resources for the well-being of the whole community and is seeking to build structures to support all children and their families. Christians are divided about this policy. Some are not happy with the state deciding what is best for individual families. Others believe that the government is doing what the church and/or its members did in the past.

Whatever your view, this is an exciting time for churches. With the Extended Schools agenda (also known as Extended Services in and around schools) churches have been recognised as potential partners, along with others, to support children and young people in their community. The phrase 'every child matters' has recently been adopted by central government and forms the basis of any partnership that might be developed between school and church.

This book explores what it might mean for Christians to work with the statutory bodies. It encourages the reader to reflect on what their local church is already doing, so that they might make the most of current opportunities to build effective partnerships within the community, especially with schools. Much of what is written is about children, but the principles apply to young people too.

The opportunities for partnerships in Scotland, N Ireland, Wales and England do vary, but the following principles and practices are broadly relevant to all education systems. You will need to adapt them to your own situation.

PART ONE – THE MOTIVATION FOR BUILDING CHURCH-SCHOOL PARTNERSHIPS

1

Government motivation – Every Child Matters

Victoria Climbié died in February 2000 after being mistreated and abused by those caring for her. Following an enquiry headed by Lord Laming, the government set up a range of measures to reform and improve children's services. Children and young people were consulted about what they wanted which led to the vision known as Every Child Matters (ECM). The five outcomes of ECM reflect what matters most to them. These outcomes are now shaping good practice for services for children and young people. For more details visit www.everychildmatters.gov.uk.

The ideal outcomes are that children and young people are:

- Healthy
- Safe
- Enjoying and achieving
- Making a positive contribution
- Achieving economic well-being

Some Christians have felt that these different areas should have included a spiritual element which has caused some local authorities to develop additional outcomes. Other Christians feel that, taken together, the original outcomes reflect the whole person and therefore already include this aspect of what it means to be human.

> **Think about...**
> Take each of the five outcomes of the ECM agenda and consider which would be met by each children and youth activity run by your church.

The situation in England

Lord Laming's Inquiry pointed out the poor co-operation between the services working with families. So new structures have been implemented to enable effective partnerships to occur naturally. Children's centres have been set up to meet the needs of families with children aged 0 to 5, many of which are attached to schools. (Once a child reaches school age, the school itself provides access to the relevant services.) By 2010, there should be 3,500 children's centres, with every state school providing access to Extended Services, developed with the active involvement of organisations (including churches) that want to be partners with the local authority, parents, carers and the community.

Extended Services is the mechanism to provide a range of services and activities that meet the needs of children in formal education and their families. This is known as the 'core offer'. Schools have been put in clusters to provide access to these core services. As Extended Services were developed, parents, children and young people have been consulted. Churches could be in a strong position to play a full part in this consultative process, to review what is needed in the community. Assuming that what a church offers to children and young people is of a high quality, schools will either signpost it to parents, adopt it in some way, or ask the church or

Christian group to work more closely with the school or even in the school. What is available will vary depending on local needs. For example, in one area schools will need to be open early to provide a breakfast club, whilst in another area a family survey may indicate this is not required. Guidance is being issued to schools about how best to engage with the voluntary sector (now known as the Third Sector).

The core offer includes four different services and is regularly updated see www.tda.gov.uk/remodelling.

- Out of school hours childcare available 8am–6pm, on weekdays, for 46 weeks of a year. Schools must provide access to a safe place for children between these hours which include a varied menu of study support activities and, in primary school, childcare opportunities.
- Parenting support
- Easy referral to specialist support services
- School facilities being available to the wider community

The situation in Northern Ireland

Schools are normally keen to build links with their local communities and welcome the involvement of local volunteers. In some areas schools are now attempting to provide facilities for children before and after the school day which provides an excellent opportunity for local church partnerships. In addition there are places for parents' and church representatives on the board of governors of every controlled school.

The situation in Wales

The emphasis has been on developing community focussed schools (an initiative known for short as CFS), to enable schools and their community to work together. For more information about ContinYou Cymru contact info.cardiff@continyou.org.uk.

The situation in Scotland

Guidance in Circular 1/2005 requires that a minimum of six Religious Observance (RO) sessions should be provided each year, in addition to traditional celebrations central to the life of the school community (such as Christmas, Easter, prize-giving). Decisions about the frequency of RO events are made by each school after consultation with the wider school community. This circular makes a distinction between Religious Observance and worship. It suggests that the most appropriate place for worship in schools is in the informal curriculum, thus making provision for Scripture Union and other Christian groups. Local churches could offer a team of people to run such groups.

In 2006, the Scottish Government passed the Parental Involvement Act, recognising that pupils learn better when parents are involved in their education and learning, welcoming parents as active participants in the life of school, as well as providing easier ways for parents to express their views and wishes. So schools are now actively looking for parents to be involved, helping out in classrooms, running voluntary clubs on school premises and taking part in the decision-making processes. All parents of pupils within a school are automatically part of a Parent Forum which decides the format, size and agenda of the Parent Council. One of the roles of the Parent Council is to promote contact between the school, parents, pupils and the community.

Church motivation

Many churches, on their own and in groups, have supported their local schools for years. This has been a natural expression of a desire to make a difference in the world, putting Bible truths into practice, especially to ensure that every child matters. Part 2 will expand on what these Bible truths mean. Currently, there are many new opportunities to

build partnerships between churches and schools, and the challenge is for churches to make the most of them. Schools are very different places from what they were, even ten years ago. Churches can celebrate the good in the past and present but also accept the challenge to see if what they offer to schools still supports what is needed. Maybe God is calling churches to do something different or in a different way.

In reality…

Members of one church regularly took assemblies in their local school. The head teacher asked if they would like to set up a café for parents. The school provided a spare classroom two afternoons a week and the church, working with other churches in the area, provided volunteers to serve tea and coffee to parents at the end of the school day.

2

PART TWO – WHAT THE BIBLE SAYS

As you would expect, the Bible says nothing directly about extended school days and the Every Child Matters agenda but that is not to say the Bible has nothing to say about these issues.

Every child matters to God

It is obvious from the exchange Jesus had with his disciples in Luke 18:15–17 that every child matters to God. The disciples rebuked mothers who had brought their children to Jesus for a blessing. But Jesus' response was, 'Let the little children come to me, and do not hinder them, for the kingdom of God belongs to such as these.' On another occasion Jesus challenged his disciples to become like a little child. 'Whoever welcomes this little child in my name welcomes me.' (Luke 9:48).

This high value placed on children runs throughout the Bible. There are many stories where children are used by God, often being asked to do difficult or important things such as Samuel, or Naaman's wife's servant girl. God's purpose for Jeremiah was set, not as an adult, but before birth (Jeremiah 1:5). Jeremiah was concerned about his age and experience, but this was no problem to God.

Think about...

On your own or with others, brainstorm the different groups of children that live in your area. How do they matter to God? Pray that God will show you what steps you could take to show them that they matter to God.

The importance of the family and the community.

We don't know much about Jesus' life as a boy but he was clearly part of his family and community. Luke 2:41–52 tells of Jesus' visit to the temple, aged 12. As Mary and Joseph travelled home, they had not noticed that Jesus was missing. They weren't negligent but his absence was attributed to his being with the wider family and friends. This would only be possible if it was a common occurrence. We can assume that it was usual for children to mix with other families, eat with them and be looked after by them.

The family of Israel as a community of people were encouraged to pass on the mighty deeds of the Lord from one generation to the next. 'Teach them to your children and to their children after them' (Deuteronomy 4:9). Moses instructed the whole community of God's people to 'impress them on your children. Talk about them when you sit at home and when you walk along the road... ' (Deuteronomy 6:7). This was something that was part of everyday life and for everyone to take on board. It is a sentiment shared by the Church of England's *All God's Children* report (1991) which concluded that 'every Christian should seek ways of witnessing to his or her faith among families and children'.

What is more, the people of Israel were required to work together for the benefit of society. Every member of society mattered. The laws given to Moses in Exodus 20 were for all; princes, nobles, freemen and slaves. When the walls of Jerusalem were rebuilt many years

Think about...
What is the vision for your church and the community around it? How does this vision have an impact on what is done with children who are already part of the church and those on the outside?

later, under the direction of Nehemiah, all members of society were encouraged to work together – different groups willingly working side by side, regardless of wealth or class (Nehemiah 3).

Children are part of the church now but, as people with a responsibility for children, we need to have a vision for the future too. (Psalm 78:4,6). The *All God's Children* report picks up on this, stating that 'everyone concerned with children should ask what sort of church and society they would like to see in 30 years' time – and what needs to be done now in order to enable that vision to be realised'.

Love God and love your neighbour

Throughout the Bible there are exhortations to love God *and* our neighbour. The Old Testament and the New Testament are in agreement as to how we should love God – with the whole of our being (eg Joshua 22:5).

Jesus confirmed just how we should love God, closely followed by the second commandment, 'Love your neighbour as yourself.' (Luke 10:25–28). The story of the Good Samaritan graphically answered the question: Who is my neighbour? This recognition of what true neighbourliness meant would have shocked Jesus' audience. Jesus was developing the message of the Old Testament with its many

exhortations for mercy and justice to be shown to foreigners living in the community. For example, Leviticus 19:34, 'the alien living with you must be treated as one of your native-born. Love him as yourself... ' This is as true today in multi-cultural Britain as it was in ancient Israel.

Being Christlike in serving others

It is always healthy to remember what sort of people we should be. Paul's uncompromising picture of Christ in Philippians 2:1–11 is as challenging as it is inspiring. Jesus is the person we are representing and therefore is the one who we are increasingly to be like. This means serving with humility and considering others and their needs above our own. Jesus embodied this when he washed his disciples' feet, acting as a servant and taking on one of the lowliest of tasks. Working with children is often looked upon as a lowly task and yet is hugely significant for the kingdom of God. As privileged sons and daughters of the King, we 'wrap towels round our waists' in whatever form of service God has called us to.

Making disciples

Just before he left his disciples, Jesus said, 'Go and make disciples of all nations… teaching them to obey everything I have commanded you.' (Matthew 28:18–20). Whatever we do as followers of Jesus Christ, whether as individuals or as part of a church community, we should be seeking to make disciples. There may be opportunities to verbally share our faith and we should be alert to this. There are certainly opportunities to demonstrate our faith. This clear mandate for the church to make disciples should be rooted in an environment where we are fully committed to enabling every child to be healthy, stay safe, enjoy and achieve, make a positive contribution and to achieve economic well-being.

3

PART THREE — PRIN(IPLE) OF GOOD PRA(TI(E

Understand your community

Whether you live in a rural village or urban city, every community is made up of smaller communities, with different needs and aspirations. Can you map out the different community groups that exist in your area, working with others in your church or other churches? You could mark the various groups onto a large map of your area. Further information is available in the 2001 census details, or visit your local authority website. Then make a list of the particular needs that you know of or feel each group may have. Match them with the vision that the church has for your area.

You would be strongly advised to discuss your findings and potential plans with the person who has been appointed by the local authority to develop such provision. Each authority has a named Extended Schools Remodelling Advisor. There will be other posts, with a variety of titles, responsible for developing Extended Services. He or she should be able to give information on local authority, school or locality plans and any needs they have already identified.

In reality...

A church located on the village high street conducted a survey of passers-by to ascertain views on the church and how people felt the church could best serve the community. This information helped to evaluate what they were doing and what else they could do.

As part of this fact-finding, pinpoint the different schools and children's centres in your local area. Find out their catchment area. The distance children travel to school will influence the types and times of possible activities. If you have identified children attending local schools in your area who are from other faiths, get hold of a copy of *Top Tips on Welcoming children of other faiths* (SU). Further ideas can be found in *Top Tips on Reaching unchurched children* (SU).

Recognise the place of schools and children's centres in the community

At one time the church was at the centre of the community with the church hall as the place for social activities for everyone, whether or not they attended church. This is less true today. The school has taken over that place in the community.

In their desire to bring about change, the government recognised that schools play a distinct role in the community. This is especially true for primary schools, since waiting at the school gate is a time for parents and carers to meet and mingle. Some have likened it to the well in Bible times, as the central meeting place in the community.

Increasingly we will find that the school or children's centre for parents of those under 5 becomes the first port of call for parents and carers. Access to childcare, family support or specialist services will be primarily through these centres. To be part of this, it is very important for churches to build strong relationships and partnerships with their local schools.

Offering 'manpower' to your local school can often be an eye-

In reality…
The Springfield Project in Sparkhill, Birmingham, a diverse multicultural community, opened as a children's centre in 2008 after a long-established programme of supporting families in the area. The local authority approached the church, to redevelop their site and provide a centre for the community (see www.springfieldproject.org.uk).

opening starting point. There are always roles to be filled; in the classroom, office, governing body or PTA. However, church premises still remain a significant resource to support initiatives that aid the community. Parent and toddler groups or nurseries often meet on church premises and provide a positive link to many local young families. In 2002 it was estimated that around 80% of work with under 5's in the UK was done on church premises.

Build trust with local schools

Schools will only work with people from a church if they trust them. Trust takes time to develop. School staff are busy with a job to do – that of educating children and young people in their care. In addition they are also expected to embrace the many new initiatives introduced by the government of the day. Staff may recognise the benefit of working with the community, both to the school itself and to individuals, but they need to see that this will be supportive, not extra work. It is vital that churches make an offer of support to a school in such a way that the school can comfortably choose to not accept it, for whatever reason.

Parents with children in the school are ideally placed to take this forward, with the potential to develop relationships and liaise with church leaders to 'build trust' in their child's school.

By recognising the particular context of schools and what their requirements are, you can ensure that the church activities complement and support what schools do. Understanding how to make links between your activities to the five outcomes of the ECM agenda and ensuring all workers running an activity in a school are CRB checked, are good starting points. Remember that any group providing Extended Services must comply with good practice guidelines which will include child protection, health and safety, food hygiene and insurance. The voluntary part of the Ofsted Childcare Register can give a helpful baseline for recognised good practice, or it could be useful to talk to the appropriate team in your local authority.

Think about...
Do you offer rewards or incentives in your voluntary group? If you reward with sweets, could you replace them with fruit or something other than food to support the school's message that encourages healthy eating? This would also demonstrate how you help children to be healthy, linking into one of the five ECM outcomes.

Grow a vision and share it with the church community

A vision for developing partnerships with the local school will emerge from the ethos of the church. Look back to Part 2 and what the Bible has to say. If the essence of what the Bible says about children, community and Christian service is being communicated regularly, the church will be expanding its vision.

The best way to turn vision into reality is usually to work with a small team, involving the church leadership, who will oversee any developments. Depending on the structure of your church, you may need to make some form of presentation to various decision-making groups, or to the church as a whole. Here are some of the issues you will need to present:

- A clear statement of what community needs you are seeking to address – for example, a neglected geographical area, a specific age group, social or educational needs (such as football coaching for under-eights, parenting classes)
- An understanding of why this is important for the church at this particular time
- Your aims and objectives (with evidence of any research you have done)
- Timescales and stages (to set up the activity and to maintain it)
- What resources (people and materials) and budget will be required (plus any funding options)
- Suggestions of what impact this might have on the church, both short and long-term

Don't expect this to be a one-off venture. People easily forget the inspiring initial motivation for a project when challenges arise, or if personal preferences need to take second place to a shared agenda.

Churches work together

The emphasis on working together across statutory, voluntary and community sectors should inspire churches to talk to each other and explore ways of working together, sharing resources as an expression of genuine Christian unity in their community. The range of possible options that a group of churches could offer is far greater than one church on its own might consider possible, especially if there is a need for long-term commitment to a regular programme.

In the most recent round of consultations with the Department of Children, Schools and Families, the government acknowledged, in what is known as the 'third sector strategy', the essential input of the voluntary sector for the success of Extended Services. It was stressed that it was important to only build partnerships with large and well-established groups who would not let schools down. On-going and consistent quality of provision is rightly required!

Think about...

Civil servants have advised some churches to work as 'churches together' presenting a large, established group with a significant human resource. This implies that schools should in fact avoid working with individual churches and encourage them to work together.

4 PART 4 - PRACTICAL IDEAS

These practical ideas are divided into two parts – school-based opportunities and community or church-based ones.

1. SCHOOL-BASED IDEAS

The provision of Extended Schools in and around school is intended, among other things, to provide out of school care for children from 8am to 6pm for 46 weeks of the year. One of the driving forces behind this initiative is to reduce child poverty. Reliable childcare means that parents who need to work can do so, knowing their children are well cared for and safe. It is also argued that such a provision can raise academic achievement, improve behaviour and lead to children and young people having better outcomes for the rest of their lives. There is no suggestion that all children should stay at school until 6pm or be forced to take part in the activities offered. Parents would be expected to pay for such a service though there may be help with these costs through tax credits. Information about such help is available through the Family Information Service that each local authority has to provide.

This provision of out of school care can create heated debate. Many Christians feel that it detracts from family life and parents should be encouraged to stay at home and care for their children rather than go to work. For many families this is neither desirable nor financially possible. Others would argue that such a provision gives all parents the choice to decide how to provide for their families. As Christians we need to be careful that when working with individual mothers or fathers we do not impose our particular view and, by so doing, make them feel guilty that they are not able to or do not want to do what we think is right. This does not stop Christians campaigning for the appropriate legislation to give parents an incentive to stay at home to care for their children.

Breakfast Club

Often held on school premises, this enables children who are dropped off early to be looked after before school. Activities would include eating breakfast and other structured pastimes, which could include listening to children read, large or small games or craft activities. Before setting up such a club, check with parents and carers that this would be welcomed and

In reality…

A church in the Scottish Borders owns a café next to the church building on the village high street. Three mornings a week, they open from 8.00am to 8.40am to serve breakfast to young people waiting to catch the bus to school. Because they offer healthy fruit and juice for free, they have secured some funding. They sell other breakfast food at cost price. It's a great opportunity for people from the church to build relationships with young people.

attended. The school may not be able to finance the running of such a club so you could make a small charge to the parents/carers. It would also be useful to talk to the local childcare team about linking costs to expenses and an overall business approach. This is likely even when you don't think you are running a business!

After-school clubs

For years, churches have been involved in running voluntary clubs in schools at lunch times or after school. The latter may or may not be held on school premises. Schools are now encouraged to provide a wide menu of activities that would be of interest to their pupils and may also support their studies. So a church-run club could be part of the core activities offered through Extended Services. Traditionally, churches have provided clubs where children have enjoyed exploring the Bible and Christianity. Scripture Union has developed the eye level range of resources, designed to work with children who have little or no knowledge of the Christian faith. For more details visit www.scriptureunion.org.uk/eyelevel

This need not be the only sort of club a church offers. Your particular talents could help children to learn or experience something new. This could open up contact with a completely different range of children and their parents. Discuss the type of clubs on offer in the school or cluster and find out how you could complement what is already on offer and be of interest. Think about costs and what would make it self-financing. For ideas on running clubs in schools, check out www.scriptureunion.org.uk/schools and www.schoolslive.org.

Holiday provision

Whilst schools have experience in providing extra-curricular activities within term time, the provision of Extended Services is all year round. In England, from 2010, all secondary schools will be expected to be open every weekday from 8am–6pm, providing access to the full core offer of services. Primary schools will not be expected to provide Extended Services on their own site but children and their families should have access to such services elsewhere. This could mean that activities you offer for children in the holidays could be signposted by the local school for parents to access. Discuss with the school and/or community what may be needed and think creatively.

Holiday provision does not have to happen on school premises but can operate in church or community premises and not just in the main holiday period either. For example, on staff training (INSET) days, parents often have to take annual leave to look after their children as these days are not always conveniently timed. During half-term holidays, especially in February and October, the weather means that children can be stuck at home. If the local authority provides a play scheme during the summer and Easter holidays you could run a church holiday club at other times. Scripture Union publishes a range of holiday club resources.

Study Support.

One of five outcomes of ECM is to enjoy and achieve and there is the expectation that schools will continue to provide extra study support for those pupils who need it. Your church could help the school meet this requirement by running homework clubs at school with appropriate supervision, or providing a study slot in the wrap-around care available. The programme of an after-school club could provide a quiet area for children to retire to when they want to do their studies. Check with the school and other churches in the area to see if it is possible to draw up a rota that enables these sessions to be run every day of the week.

After-school sport

Schools are encouraged to increase the amount of sport offered both within and outside the school day. The new offer, called the '5 hour sport offer', is aimed at 'semi-sport' types; those who like sport but would never make a school team. Two hours a week are to be provided  in school-time with three hours available out of school, two of which should be in a competitive environment. Does your church have members who could run a football, cricket or tennis club at school? Could churches run a five-a-side league? What church-based leagues or tournaments already exist that could be modified to meet this need? Check out Christians in Sport for further advice www.christiansinsport.org.uk.

YFC *The Crux*

In response to the need to make high quality study support materials available for schools, Youth for Christ has produced *The Crux*. This is a daily study support programme (over a three year cycle) written from a Christian perspective, covering key curriculum areas over five days – IT, sport, the arts, citizenship and spirituality. Sessions are fully scripted and come with a how-to DVD. They are designed to be used by teachers or volunteers. *The Crux* has been recognised as an excellent resource by civil servants and Extended Schools experts. Intended for secondary schools, three of the five streams are useable with key stage 2 (sport, the arts and citizenship). For more information contact thecrux@yfc.co.uk.

Computer Club

A computer club for pupils, parents or families has lots of potential. Most schools have computer suites and it may be possible to partner with them to create an opportunity for pupils to complete homework assignments or practise skills after school. Is there a need in the wider community to help adults gain computer skills needed for the job market? Does your church have members who could run short courses for adults? This would meet the aims of Extended Services by providing for the community as well as creating an opportunity to meet people you may never meet elsewhere.

Times of transition

It is recognised that there is a need to support children and young people at times of transition, whether on starting school, moving from primary to secondary school, or making decisions about what happens at age 16. Scripture Union has published the book *It's your move* for those in transition from primary to secondary school, which has been available for over seven years. Churches often make a gift of *It's your move* to their local school(s) and also take assemblies or run workshops, and even residential short holidays, to help prepare students to move to secondary school. There are also books for families when children initially enter school (*Get, ready, go*) and for young people as they make choices at the end of their school career (*Life actually*). For more details see page 31.

The government has also recognised that times of transition are not easy and for some families even choosing which nursery or secondary school to apply for is very daunting. Churches could support families and students making such choices. Talk to the school and local authority to find out if there is a need for these services which are not provided by other agencies. Decide what you can and want to do. Visit www.scriptureunion.org.uk/families for suggestions on running an event on 'Making choices biblically – how to choose a secondary school'. Think about how you can use *It's your move*.

Schools are always looking for ways to offer additional options, so often welcome gifts of resources that churches might offer. Sets of books such as *It's your move* are one possibility. Another gift might be *Into the Bible*, a programme of a class set of books containing 101 Bible extracts laid out in a child-friendly format. This also includes a CD-ROM containing 24 lesson outlines for KS2 with everything for a teacher to deliver a Bible-focused lesson that is tied in with the requirements of local RE syllabi. For more details visit www.scriptureunion.org.uk/intothebible.

2. COMMUNITY AND CHURCH-BASED IDEAS

Supporting parents

Extended Services is not just about providing childcare for children or improved examination results but is an initiative that aims to meet the needs of the whole family. One of the strands is specifically about supporting parents. It is not just every child that matters but every parent matters too, as the government document *Every Parent Matters* explains – see www.teachernet.gov.uk/everyparentmatters.

In reality…
In one community in N Ireland, a Mothers' Union parenting facilitator piloted a group in a school for parents to meet for discussion and learning together. The Mothers' Union are keen to repeat this project elsewhere in N Ireland.

Opportunities to support parents could include parenting classes, support for dads or parents with children who have special needs, single parents, language classes, toddler groups. Before deciding to offer a service, check with the families and schools in your area if what you are proposing is wanted and not available elsewhere. As far as possible, co-operate with other churches.

Visits to schools/Life path

Churches have worked together in running day-long events for primary children in a local historical site – such as a monastery, cathedral or priory. During the day they explore the life path of the relevant saint, significant Christian or community, the life path of Jesus and how this might relate to their own life path. This connects with the requirements of local syllabi for Religious Education. For more details visit www.scriptureunion.org.uk/lifepath.

Christians have often been welcomed into schools to lead assemblies, take RE lessons or participate in Religious Observance sessions in Scotland or to be a visitor who shares their faith, as recommended in the national guidelines for the teaching of RE.

Another means of supporting the teaching of RE is for churches to welcome classes of children to the church premises. This may be to explore features of the church's architecture or may be a seasonal workshop, often Easter or Christmas.

Local trust model

As things become more established, it may be practical to set up structures to sustain a longer-term community-wide work. Where churches join forces, usually one has to give more of a lead and take on some of the financial and legal responsibilities. An alternative model is to set up a local trust through which churches can work together. Many communities have done this successfully and Scripture Union runs an Associate Scheme to support local trusts. This can help deal with the various processes to clarify aims and objectives, setting up a trust, issues related to employing a worker and accessing suitable training and support. For more details see www.scriptureunion.org.uk/associates or www.suscotland.org.uk/regional/associate_staff.html.

Networks

There are a growing number of networks that connect those interested in building up partnerships between church and school. They provide information, training programmes and resources. *Children Matter!* is a coalition of individuals and organisations wanting to strengthen the Christian response to children in the UK. Through the website there is a regular newsfeed, downloadable resources and a growing number of local and specialised networks that you can join, or even initiate. For more details visit: www.childrenmatter.net.

TEN TOP TIPS:

- Pray (now and throughout!)

- Get to know and understand your community

- Discuss with others in your church the nature of the church's role in the community

- Work with other churches to explore ideas

- Get to know your local schools and Extended Schools Remodelling Advisor

- Be familiar and keep up to date with the Every Child Matters agenda and make regular visits to government department websites, especially www.dcsf.gov.uk

- Wherever possible, look for projects that strengthen partnership with others

- Look for what resources are available to support you

- Reflect on the way that your vision or activity best fits the needs of the community

- Be prepared to change as needs and opportunities emerge

RESOURCES

Resources and Supporting Bodies:

www.surestart.gov.uk – Sure Start is the government's programme to deliver the best start in life for every child by bringing together early education, childcare, health and family support.

www.everychildmatters.gov.uk

www.teachernet.gov.uk/wholeschool/extendedschools

www.tda.gov.uk/remodelling – for information on how extended services are rolled out.

www.cabinetoffice.gov.uk/third_sector – for information on how government wants to develop relationships with the Third Sector (which used to be called the voluntary sector).

www.4children.org.uk – the national charity dedicated to creating opportunities and building futures for all children.

www.dcsf.gov.uk – the department for children, schools and families.

www.scotland.gov.uk/topics/education/schools

www.schoolswork.co.uk

www.youthwork.co.uk

www.scriptureunion.org.uk; www.suni.co.uk; www.suscotland.org.uk

In Schools: www.scriptureunion.org.uk/schools

Associate Scheme: www.scriptureunion.org.uk/40353.id

It's Your Move: www.scriptureunion.org.uk/itsyourmove

Training in schools work course – contact: rutht@scriptureunion.org.uk

Eyelevel and midweek club resources:
www.scriptureunion.org.uk/eyelevel

Into the Bible (RE resource): www.scriptureunion.org.uk/intothebible

Life path: www.scriptureunion.org.uk/lifepath

Families support: www.scriptureunion.org.uk/families

Other useful websites

www.childrenmatter.net – see page 29
www.urbansaints.org
www.spurgeonschildcare.org – Spurgeon's Network was launched in 2007 as a specialist network for those involved in Christian childcare in the UK and connects into the annual Christian Childcare Forum.
www.christianchildcareforum.org.uk – is about making links between practitioners across the 'looked after children' sector as well as those more concerned with church-based children and youth work.
www.yfc.co.uk/resources/thecrux – The Crux, an extended schools resource with 60 interactive sessions providing an innovative professional secondary and primary school programme for every day of the school year.
www.ci2eye.co.uk – ci2eye exists to link and support Christian work specifically in early years' education.
www.continyou.org.uk – a leading community learning charity.

Printed resources

Midweek club resources from Scripture Union include the following eyelevel resource programmes: *Streetwise, Awesome, Clues2Use, Rocky Road, High Five and Target Challenge*. For all details of SU children's programmes visit www.scriptureunion.org.uk
Sue Radford, Jill Rowe and Jenny Baker, *Generation to Generation*, Scripture Union, 1999 (This is a most useful book if you are not already involved.)
What makes for good partnership, Shaftsbury Society/Faithworks
Phil Bowyer, *Express community through schools – Taking social action beyond the classroom*, Authentic Media, 2007